The Land Behind the Eyes

By

B. Brunswick

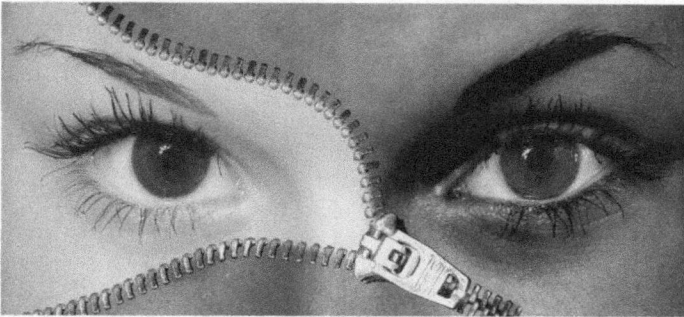

ISBN: 978-0-6452266-0-7

Dedication

To Mum:
You're the one who stood by me and supported me no matter what I went through or put you through. For that, I am eternally grateful.

A special mention for Kat (Pickle) and Zee for inspiration, friendship, support, laughs and a million other things. Thank you!

Acknowledgments

I would like to thank my cover designer Tracey at Soxsational Cover Art for doing a wonderful job once again. I know I'm difficult, sorry!

I would also like to thank J.S. Larmore for her editing skills and most importantly, her friendship. You have an understanding of me and my words that no other could match. I am forever grateful and appreciate all that you are, more than you could ever know.

http://jslarmore.com/services

Warning

This book contains bad language

Contents

Introduction

Close your eyes. What do you see?

The colours and patterns of your own existence, the pictures and the memories. A world behind the eyes. Where you are one in your you-ness. Where you can fool yourself into darkness or convince yourself of your light. It's the place we must search the most when looking for our answers. Many times, those answers come from within. A world not just of thought, but of emotions, heart, spirit and soul.

Each of us is at the centre of our own personal universe in **The Land Behind the Eyes**

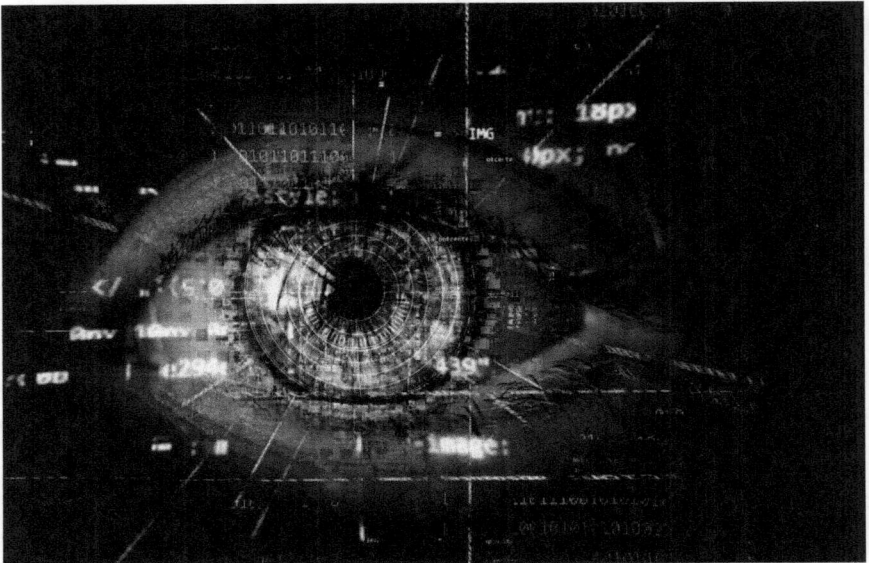

The Land Behind the Eyes

From the depth of deepest blackness
The colours endless swirling
Flashes skip from pink to purple
The wall of rainbow towering

The sunflower appears so often
Like a symbol floating freely
I am falling, I am running
I am in my mind completely

The animals that whisper
And the faces ever morphing
They're there and then forgotten
In yet another misty morning

Florescent, effervescent
With no reality to cling
No feeling on my body
No sunshine and no wind

The tunnel that surrounds me
Unto a field of golden grass
The golden rabbit's here to greet me
The rainbow one just passed

The smiles through the tubes of colour
The purple blob that leaves my stare
The shadow creeps across the ceiling
The flower fields that aren't quite there

Twisting, turning, changing, forming

The shallow stream, the ocean wide
Till I reach the sunlit morning
I am the land behind the eyes

The Strong One, the Weak One

You are the strong one
The old and the wise
You've got the answers
No chance of demise
You are the answer
The hope and the prayer
You are hope for the broken
You are flying out there
You are the chosen
Help the sick and the lame
You may be chosen
But you're always blamed
You are the winner
You can win over hearts
You're the best winner
You can cover the scars
You are the joker
The clown and the tramp
You are the dick head
The ignored and the damned
You are the wonder
That untucks us all
You are the stupid, the clown and the fool.
You are the everything
The light in the dark
You are the forgiven
The walk in the park
You are the wisdom
You are the pain
You are the stumble
Each time and again

You are the surging
That the others will fear
You hang onto nothing
But hold freedom so near
You are the soft word
To the broken, the lame
But you will fall short
Time and again
You are the future
That is stuck in the past
You're not the first
You will not be the last
You are the cold calling
The bringer of sin
You'll never keep crying
If your dust in the wind
You are the sweet nothing
With nothing to fear
You won't fall the fuck over
But you may shed some tears
You are the starlight surveyor
The hole in a heart
The fucked and the lonely
The cold and the dark
You're constantly craving
That something to taste
The darkness closes in
Like a slap to the face
You are the strained voices
You struggle to hear
They'll throw you away
When they should pull you near
You are the illusion

The shit in the lake
You're a ball of confusion
And a fuckin' mistake
You suck all the fibres
Til the cosmos is bare
Your hole growing wider
The longer your hair
You are so violent
With no will to fight
An old lonely head
And the feelings collide
You hand out forgiveness
Like an axe to the head
You wanna come on the journey
You don't know what's next
You are the strong one
But you don't know the way
Even the strongest one
Can be weak for a day

The Land Behind the Eyes 7

You, the One True Enemy

Do you know where you're headed?
Is there doubt you can reach it?
Do the walls hang vertical, jagged and daunting over your head?
Do memories drift by, never changing, looking backwards at the
things you once did?
Yesterday shouldn't be forgotten, it isn't, it's there
Hanging in the background, making you weak, haunting like
dark spirits and making you cry out loud
Knees sore from begging for forgiveness, from a demon in your
mind
Immersed in blood that douses the flames of even the sweetest
reason
A hurricane lurks, it follows you raging along the path to
anywhere
It wants to mess up your clothes, your shelter, and maybe even
your existence
Scurrying through tunnels, round mazes, in a million labyrinths
of decisions
The choices are endless, but many lead to nowhere at all, and
some to your downfall
Creeping round corners, afraid to step out into the light
The light lives inside you, so does the shadow, so does the clown,
the warrior, the beast and the fool
Fighting it out to surface, to feed off your doubt, your fear, or
your laughter, or your strength
Purge the fear, surge forward, taking arrows in your rhino skin
Let the blood pour from the wounds, let it make you warm, let it
make you smile

Taking a kick out of failing, taking a lump out of pain, seeking
endless, not the meaning but the feeling
Snakes will hide in the grass, glassy eyes staring, forked tongue
flicking tasting you, their prey
Twisting reason and turning your pathetic weapons upon
yourself
Making you wear a mask, making you hide, making you quiet
Now is not the time to shut up, now is the time to scream
Now is the time to roar your battle cry, the one that makes the
cold killers of the jungle quake in their boots
Now is the time to surge forward and break on through
To march one-minded, towards a destiny that could be yours
To grow courage, to grow a backbone, to grow an iron skin
To leave the bad memories and the shitsy moments, silent and
staring and jealous of what you've become
The reasons to hate yourself are no longer valid
You can grow above and beyond them, those shackles that you
were born into
They feel like steel, but those chains are made of glass
That will shatter in shards and drop to the ground and sparkle
like glitter in the golden sunlight
The crystal mirrors, that showed a face, pained, cracked and
aging
Can show a face beautiful, and smiling and loving the skies, the
oceans, the forests, or the mountains behind it
Only now do you see them
They've always been there
You are the one, the joyous one, the loving one, the weever of
dreams, the crafter of memories
The stone-like statue you dwell within is crumbling, it wants to

hold on, but there came a time when you didn't need it anymore
Now is the time to be you
The choices are yours
This life is yours
You, the one true enemy
Or you, your own best friend

Vacant

The crumbled soul is vacant
Shattered, falling, like shards of glass
The instant desolation
Battered calling, so blind, so dark
The destiny is boulders
Harrowing, and towers tall
The weight upon your shoulders
They're narrowing, to make you fall
The temperature is rising
Burning, a red monster on the hunt
The pain you feel surprising
Learning, by now you should be numb

When you think it's the destination
It's morphing, it moves again
Endless desperation
Mind warping, the empty end
Pretend you smile widely
Cleansing, hoping to dry your eyes
You stumble forward blindly
Pretending, you're not as cold as ice
It's gnawing endless at your soul
Flesh ripping, the blood is spilt
It's drawing you friendless in the hole
You're tripping upon the flood of guilt

Bottle's running empty
Swaying down the narrow beam
Throttled through the century
Try praying but you don't believe
Greyness in the skies again

Dark clouds, and the howling wind
So weary, stinging in the rain
Heart pounds, the breath it thins
Tasting freedom that you dreamed of
Exuded the grains of truth
Ever breathing, never screamed off
Excluded from the rains of youth

It's a moment, it's not forever
Joy flows if you can light the dark
It's just holding it together
Who knows, just trust your heart
It's reaching out for someone
Share love, and smile inside
It's teaching what is dear
Lifted up and you'll survive
The hope for hope not over yet
So spaced out, so lost in life
The hope of hope lies up ahead
Pain fades out, it just takes time

The Responsibility of Hearts

You hold my heart, be you friend, be you lover
You hold a piece of my ever-giving soul
You catch my eyes, the thoughts inside my mind
You've won my love, and I give my heart to you to hold

I give my trust. I give my belief for you forever
Come stand by me. Come here and I'll protect you
I don't want this barricade. You don't have to wear a mask
My soul runs deeply, and my faith burns true

And the pain will come, the dark days always get us
But we'll stand with pride and together we'll be stronger
You can hold me up, that's why I chose to need you
Whether for a fleeting moment, for a fleeting life or fleeting ever
longer

Smiles can fill the day, and laughter fill the misty evening
And the joy will come in rolling waves across the bay
And in they crash, explode, frothy on the shoreline
But after a few lingering seconds they get sucked back to an
endless ocean's freedom far away

Whether we have sang songs, or walked the streets together
If we've spent the years, shared a tear, or danced together for a
night
Our connected souls the mysterious cosmos brought together
You passed you're love to me and I sent back a glowing flow, a
bucketful of mine

If you give your love, your friendship, and your heart to me
I have a duty and a drive to look after it, and hold it precious
from the start
The lies and spite I do not know, I'll make mistakes, but my
intentions always noble
I'd never mean to hurt you, it's my pride, it is my honour, it's my
life—The responsibility of hearts

Smiles

When the Earth, it rumbles
Or in the howling wind
When all the strength just crumbles
And a shadow looms within
When the rage and hate surround you
When the spite leaves a bitter taste
When your fate skirts right around you
Or spits venom in your face
When the love leaves you abandoned
When there's no hope up ahead
When the mind is cold and saddened
And there's demons in your head
When there's red eyes in the tree line
When the storm is rolling in
When it stalks you like a feline
When it hurts, or bites, or stings
When your silent in the cold night
Or lonesome in the day
When the suffering of a lifetime
Won't ever seem to go away
When you're frozen or are stranded
When you've lost the weary path
When by the darkness you're surrounded
And your ever-broken heart
When you've always got a struggle
Up the ever-steepening hill
When you're tripping on the rubble
And feel you're standing still

When the legs are surely straining
And the pain won't seem to end
When it's freezing and it's raining
I still love you my sweet friend

The Good Souls

I dreamt I'd forgotten about the world
Drifting through the misty tunnels of time
The world that held no rhyme or reason
The journey that had no reason or rhyme

The nightshade captures the silver moonlight
Falling through colours, intense and alive
Silent and gentle and floating on nothing
In imagery of confusion, on the illusions you thrive

Talking whispers that sneak in the eardrums
The jumbled and bumbled, pictures so free
The jaws of the night are clinging your conscious
The fools of the truth are invading your dreams

Take every message from every passage of wisdom
Talking you down, from a place that's so high
Your mind is flipping, you're reaching for freedom
The price that you pay is the time to survive

Keep pushing on and remember keep breathing
Keep spreading truth, the lessons you've learned
Keep spreading love like butter on freedom
Keep telling them the words that the good souls have earned

The Fight of Life

Keep fighting
Never quit
You'll need your spirit
Your drive and grit
They fear you
They're talking shit
Keep rolling
Each and every hit

Keep dreaming
To touch the stars
The wounds heal
And just leave scars
Keep pushing
Keep moving fast
Keep growing
Until the last

You'll stumble
Fuck, don't we all?
You'll stumble
But you won't fall
Keep breathing
Keep standing tall
It won't stop you
If you can knock down walls

Without darkness
We wouldn't know night
It hurts you
It's not fair, not right

Come morning
You'll feel the light
It's happened
But it's not your life
You're not quitting
You'll stand and fight

The Cave

Skulking silent in the shadows
The lingering wall of dark
The inkiness greedily swallows
And blackens the cold heart

The cave in its jagged mouth
The darkness dwells within
The constant need to pull you near
Sitting fuckin' quaking, in the stinging wind

Skeletons can taunt you
And try to fuck your life
Forever do they stab it in
And then twist the fuckin' knife

The shadow yearns to eat you
It wants to consume your soul
It loves nothing more than to see you crumbled
And writhing in that you-sized hole

Your burning torch evades you
And the walls come clanging round
The sky is smoke, and glowing ash
The shadow's smiling on the ground

Glimmers of sweet nothing
The only time you get
When there's a hundred million other things
Running like a movie in your fuckin' head
The shadows they will be there
They are there forever more
But in the hands of time, they fade away

And make you stronger to the core

The shadows they can never win
If you don't give up the fight
Come out of the cave, explore the world
Take a step towards the light

Lost

Stare empty at the hollow reflection in the shattered mirror
Jaded, dragging your existence across the shards of glass
The blood pours from your feet, the tears pour from your soul,
the shadows pour from your being
Voices that echo through time, ever twisting their meaning, until
they take flight and drift off alone
Depression looms in the future, its darkness inviting, just as it
lingers in the past
Holding on, gripping your very soul, dragging you back, pulling
you to where you belong
You know the path, but this one is covered in ice, you slip and
slide along it, towards a destiny of hope
You fade out, lonely, spent all your goodness on folly pursuits,
on rescuing those who refuse to rescue themselves
Silence is deafening as you claw the walls, testing your
boundaries, seeing if you can snap
Tears roll down pale cheeks, threatening to drown out the joy
The joy, the hope, the freedom that you dared to dream of, that
you dared to taste, all gone
The moment of darkness comes raining down again, blackening
your heart, validating your misery, validating your sense of worth
Your worth feels nothing, but bad memories pouring into your
flooded soul
Hatred looms, it's deadly and certain and creeping
Slipped false smiles that fall from your face and roll around
stricken on the ground
Whispers from the smiling faces of the past, that once brought
you warmth now haunt you
They echo through the silent moments as you stare out to
nothing, wrapped within your dream
Sullen fingers of decaying grief invade your being and linger

Fighting through a howling wind, as it rips at your hair and
gouges out your eyes
Spirits wallow in swamps of pity, thick with stinking mud
They cruelly carry you backwards, to the place from which you
came, the place from which you narrowly escaped with yourself
Bringing back the fear and the hopelessness, and the
worthlessness again
Though you know too well it never leaves, just dampens in times
of warmth
Thoughts so scary, emotions even scarier
Laughter maniacal, but masked, and muffled so it never becomes
real
But the fear of this place doesn't mean it's not comfort, doesn't
mean that's not how you've always existed
Stuck in that place
While forgetting
That place you have escaped from, you can do it once again, each
time remembering the way back into the light
Each time it becomes easier as you grow stronger
It may try and beat you down
But you will overcome
You're spiralling forward and downwards into what despair has
left behind
But you are not finished
You are just for a moment, lost

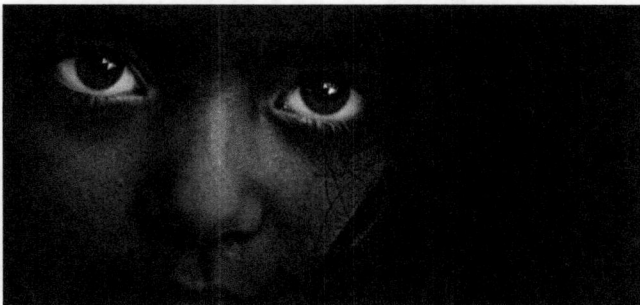

Senses

I felt the savage rumble, I felt the bitter tear
I saw them falling and then weeping and yes, I felt the fear

I heard the lost souls screaming, I heard the creatures cry
I heard them die frozen, at that moment, if they weren't strong
enough to fly

I saw the blood that stained the cold sheets, saw long lost
longing eyes
I saw them shaking, fuckin' screaming, and yes, I heard the cries

I smelled the far long frozen reason, I smelled the bitterness, the
grief
I saw it all unfolding but I stared on, cold, in disbelief

I tasted bitter armies, that had tasted such defeat
I tasted the hate of humans, it didn't taste too sweet

I felt the shadows ever-forming, I felt the loneliness so dear
I felt the beast was coming home soon, and yes, I felt the fear

I heard the ravers ever-ramble, heard the others just sit tight
I heard you cry into your pillow, I heard you lose the fight

I saw the pity circle gently, I saw the light just fading out
I saw your world that fell and crumbled, I saw the bitter seeds of
doubt

I smelled just like a coward, I smelled the bullshit flying round
I smelled the truth that's coming forward and it's never falling
down

I tasted dreary lonesome Mondays, I tasted pain that would make
you cringe
I tasted empty frozen shadows, like a hurricane within

I felt silly, I felt wasted, I felt lost and never here
I felt a million warriors, and yes, I felt their fear

I heard a ditty and a melody, and I heard a soul alive
I heard them singing, talking, laughing, heard them forget about
the time

I saw an endless cold horizon, saw a mountain in my way
I saw the howling wind that caught my tongue, left me nothing
else to say

I smelled the horse shit and the empty, I smelled the doubt inside
their heart
I smelled the truth and jumped through hoops, but forgot about
the start

I tasted happiness, a silent bliss, when I'm standing on my feet
And you will fall one more time if you never tame the beast

I felt the moans and storms unknown, felt a whisper in my ear
I felt them shiver down my spine, and yes, I felt the fear

Inside

The pain, the scars, the tears, the wars
The bitter cloud of grief
The doubt, the lies, the truth, the cause
The crumpled in a heap

The sights, the smell, the cries of fear
The walls that crumbled down
Forgotten, frozen, ripped apart
The fog that lingers round

The anger, the hate, the spite, the roars
The helplessness, the violence
The long cold night, the ripping claws
The suffering in silence

The twists, the turns, the lessons learned
The sorrow and the guilt
The shadow that's been hanging round
Pushes on you like a quilt

The yells, the hurt, the fire burns
To scorch the soul to ash
The broken hearts, the wind will turn
And then hit you in a flash

The storms, the hail, the raging waves
The ship drifting out to sea
The shackles that keep us here a slave
And longing to be free
The treading through the mud so thick
That's pulling on your feet

The worry of the little things
To never get to sleep

Tear a hundred hearts apart
And walk on through your pain
Shudder stop, before the start
Getting ripped up by the rain

The ghosts that walk the dusty hall
The horrors and the crime
The monsters try to make you fall
They wanna make you die

Till the body bulges with the time
The scars build up within
And he may look like he's made of stone
But it lives inside of him

Being Here

The light that we walk through, yet fail to see
The core of the journey, adventures through dreams
The moment we cling to, torn wide apart
The consciousness drifting, the words from the heart
The ledge-way so narrow, maybe too narrow to cross
Are we searching for something or just getting lost?
Dynamic, still breathing, still yelling aloud
Stumbling journey with each step we are proud
Voicing our grievance and the other one's cold take
Swimming for freedom, just another mistake
Echoes like thunder downtrodden the path
Finishing first means not finishing last
Prison can trap but it's a chance to escape
Sew up once more that lonely heartbreak
Taking the time to see through the dust
We're loyal and brave and unapologetically us
The mind can play tricks the mind sometimes taunts
Picking the fights and not winning the wars
Climbing an ice sheet, pissing in wind
We know where we're standing, but not where we've been
Standing, staggering, stammering, still
Swallowing pride like a huge bitter pill
Gravity can be heavy, crushing your bones
Crowded, surrounded but completely alone
The cliff ever looming, hangs over the head
Keep crawling, keep moving, til you're cold and you're dead.
Fight for the meaning, distant unclear
Creeping and crawling and screaming in fear
Happy to linger on a conundrum unknown
Searching for warmness, searching for home
The feelings bombard us, like the sun's cosmic rays

The minds getting better, but the body it fades
Scraping a living from a pot of fuck all
The big, they grow bigger, while wanting us small
Distracted, and lost and dwell in the sorrow
The promise of sunshine to meet you tomorrow
Keeps us from lingering and sniffing the flowers
Hanging around going stagnant for hours
Tip the hat to the morning, raise hands to the night
Swaying so gently in the moon light so bright
Is the point of the reason to not live in fear?
To live out the dreams, not just being here

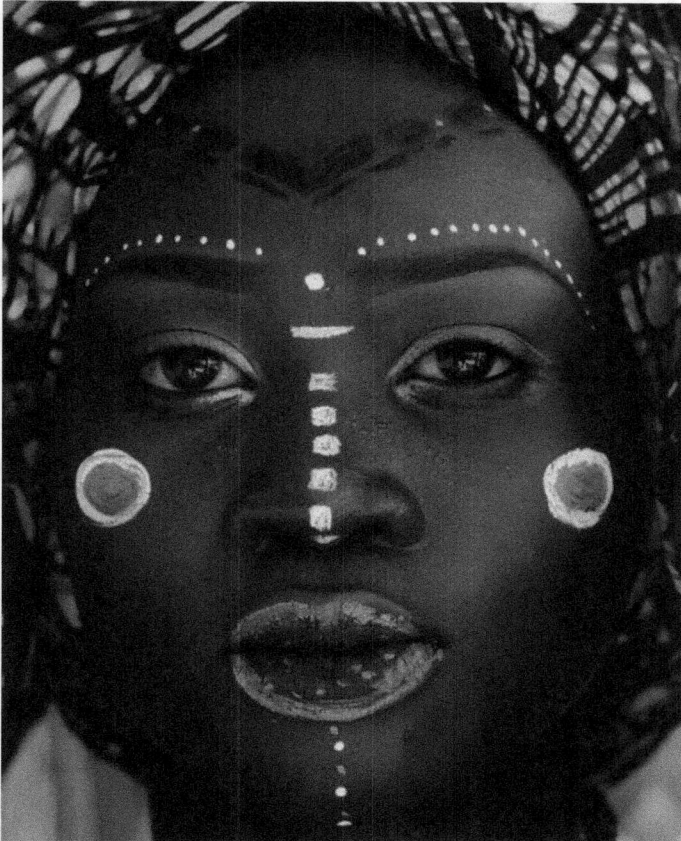

The Child Unborn

The spirit is floating, divided and swaying
Like crystal memories swooping through nowhere
Flying through dreams and beautiful colours
Deep into the world that's not there

Whatever your seeing, living or breathing
The soul wanders through galaxies twinkling and far
And a whisper of existence, is telling and choosing
Who, what, why, when or where that you are

The consciousness considers existence unknowing
Drifting through thought if never drifting through life
Silence surrounding, the halls lead to sleeping
Never doubting the truth, never knowing what's right

Never dreaming, or sleeping, unknown, unbelieving
Still creeping through a silent shadow in your mind
Never silent or weeping, like a wisp of steam in the wind
Never burn angry, never fire like the rage in your eyes

You're the child unborn, your spirit and soul are unmade
But it doesn't mean that you're not out there and true
Maybe you wait for your moment, patiently, forever
To become a life that is born, to become the wonder that's you

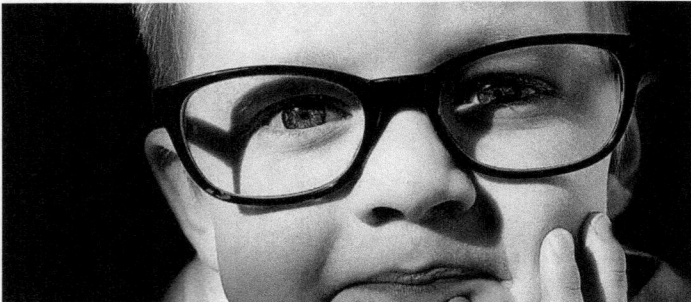

A Bad Day

There's love circling
It doesn't enter this hole
Storm clouds loom above
But the warmth doesn't enter this soul
Reaching out
To nothing, invades
When you don't have the hope
The comfort evades
There's a small person
Overlooked and untasked
Who means nothing to no one
The questions unasked
There's a dark cloud
Drifting the sky
Trying hard to break you
Trying to make you cry
There's a forgotten person
On the end of the line
But no one will answer
No joy to define
There's a shallow grave
Dug and prepared
Wanting to break you
Wanting you to be scared
There's a cracked face
In the reflection to see
Crumbled and imprisoned
No chance to be free
There's a shadow ahead
But it feels like it's home
Grabbing your reason

Leaves you standing alone
There's a whisper
That floats on the breeze
It talks to the mountains
The rivers, the trees
There's a broken bridge
Across a chasm so wide
That taunts you and fucks you
And wills you inside
There's a dark cave
Of pity, of spite
You so wish to enter
It will swallow the light
There's a bad choice
Between giving and lost
When the gravity's heavy
And you're dropping your cross
There's a mere dream
That means nothing to most
That fucks with your fortune
And screws with your ghost
There's a deep ocean
And you're lost on the sea
Drifting and lonesome
In a bid to be free
There's a bad day
There's another again
The wind it is howling
The silence your friend
There's a dead no one
That nothing will grieve
When you wear your black heart
On the tatty old sleeve

There's an emptiness
It comes to find you once more
And your heart breaks like waves
On the jagged cold shore
There's a watery strength
That can't hold the weight
You wish you could run from
But you can't escape
There's a cracked old body
And a roadway of scars
That you travel on legs
After crashing your car
There's a tunnel
Across the kingdom's divide
Strangling the fuck out of you
But it won't let you die
There's thunder
That rattles your heart
There's a goal to reach
But nowhere to start
There's moments
There's hours that waste
And the light that you miss
Lost in the bad days

Lizard Skin

You're sitting there hunched over, all wrapped in lizard skin
You're crooked cold and broken, a bitterness within
Your misguided stupid frozen, you're spitting out the spite
You're so blinded by your hatred, you don't know what is right

Your beauty here is wasted, your sparkle cannot shine
Wrapped inside your lizard skin and fucked in your own mind
Your eyes fixed upon your victim, slashing with your teeth
While your poison slowly kills them, makes them frail, makes
them weak

The howling wind across you, the wasted in your wake
The howling wolf inside you, that cannot get their way
The thunder without lightning, the red-faced fuckin' rant
The anger, you let it fuel you, you stupid little man

Ever thought of loving, or maybe being nice?
Ever thought of chilling out and stop the fuckin' fight?
And you're living in the desert, like a lizard in the wind
But if he sees the beauty then the lizard sheds his skin

Come Outside

Come outside, into the light
The time has come to show you're brave
The darkness holds you trembling inside
The shadows dwell within your cave

The dark won't leave, always there
Feeds greedily off your screams
The only way is to step outside
And stumble towards your waking dreams

The forks of doubt, the jagged smirk
The sly stabbing wicked at your soul
The creatures howl, the haggard lurk
Drag you kicking and screaming into your hole

The mists of fear, that dangle black
The edge of winter leaves a chill
The memories long to take you back
To leave you frozen, standing still

And all once you dare to dream
Beyond the hate, beyond the lies
Come outside, into the light
With that magic in your eyes

Skipping Stones

The planets keep moving
The endless in motion
The marvel magnificent and grand
Things are confusing
As the tumbling ocean's
Great waves lick away on the sand
Stealing back the rock and the land

Memories whispers
Will trigger emotions
That will hang around your soul for too long
Consciousness drifters
At one with the notion
That we search for where we belong
While we're skipping like stones on a pond

While we have momentum
Drive and devotion
The luxury of time to grow and to think
We look through the spectrum
Ignoring commotion
While we wander a razor-like brink
When it's all just too easy to sink

Every second so fleeting
Another lost moment
Another day flies away on the wind
Just gotta keep breathing
And rub on the lotion
Of your crumbling layer of thick skin
And the warmth and protection it brings

Memories blisters
Will hold the emotions
That have hung in your soul for too long
Brothers and sisters
At peace with the notion
That we'll find the place we belong
While we're skipping like stones on a pond

Seeing the Stars

The clouds rolled above me
The shadows around me
I hurt til the hurt was the norm
I fought every moment
Both naked and frozen
Through the wild, raging wind and the storm
The waves smashed the shoreline
Red eyes in the tree line
Like cold jagged fingers dragging me down
Breaking my being
Constantly fleeing
From the sad, from the fucked on the ground
The hours were endless
Suffered relentless
I carry the pain and the scars
I was puffing and blowing
I was lost and unknowing
And at last, I am seeing the stars

I was forgotten and empty
I was dreaming so gently
Of things that I never could reach
I wasn't deserving
It was scary, unnerving
And I rolled like a wave on the beach
Life was a journey
I followed so blindly
Like I never had any choice
I was shouting my fury
Not dreaming of glory
Losing my mind and my voice

The tears so long falling
The pain it kept calling
Breaking my soul and my will
I was sitting there starving
Breaking, yet laughing
And I didn't even know how to feel
I've walked the long journey
And though this life burned me
I learned to live the days like your last
And I been on the edge now
Hung off the ledge now
And at last, I am seeing the stars

The pain didn't take me
It never could break me
But it took me as far as it could
I felt so frustrated
But the man that I hated
Was one that was strong, kind and good
Putting my focus
Away from the hopeless
I put it to feeling so free
I found what I needed
Then sweating and bleeding
I fought down to the truth that is me
I never quite failed
When the wind left my sails
I never put my head in my hands
And often I struggled
Over history's rubble

But I always managed to stand
Now I take what I'm earning

Everyday I'm still learning
I have only just realised my path
I've learned of my duty
I'm seeing the beauty
And at last, I am seeing the stars

The Human

A disappearing meaning when this shield you wear crumbles
Stumbling, falling, on the journey into the non-existent existence
Talking your heart out into ears that refuse to hear a word
Blowing your mind out and dodging sweet and steady reason like
the plague
Rampant with hatred, it's just the human about us, it's just what
we are
Growling, while the beast comes out to play for a while
Smiling like a crazy person at the moon, will it acknowledge us?
Creeping like a spy, full to the brim with the dread of resistance
The existential mindset, clanging like shadows in the cage of the
mind
You can be empty, you can be foolish, you can be as lonesome as
a seed adrift on the wind
Do you care?
No second chances, no memories, seek forgiveness by a sword to
your throat
The blood thirsty are prowling, they want you, they want that
wanderer's soul
You roll through existence like thunder rumbling in the distance
The lightning within you alights like the clouds
Killers and thieves and doubters are living amongst us
The warfare keeps raging in our being, but beyond our sight
Rainbows and their beauty, they sparkle, but they blind us
The cosmos is breathing, dreaming of the connection to us
Stars exploding, sending shockwaves through our DNA, the very
grain of our being
Life can drag you away like the foaming rapids, surging down the
river wild
It can leave us cold, it can leave us vacant, it can leave us
standing, shuddering still

Take up a hobby that's pointless, or stare into the abyss of the
colours flashing across the screen
"Keep them entertained. Keep them distracted." Works so
fucking well when we'd rather bury our heads in the sand.
We're outraged, we're astounded, we're confused, we're puppets
and slaves
Carrying weapons doesn't give us freedom, real freedom is when
we no longer want or need to
Real freedom is wandering the Earth without fences, walls or
boundaries
Real freedom is not thinking outside the box, it's not being put
inside a box at all
Running into illusions over and over, keeping our lives mundane,
keeping us average
Teaching us to envy and fear that which is not ours, making us
feel we could never achieve what they did
They are lucky, or maybe they are special, or maybe they're just
another you, in another reality
Wishing always for what we can't have, unsatisfied by the taste
of the bitter fruit
Spending every ounce of gold that our blood produced, just to
make us feel we are better than we really are
Everyone is watching our every move, eager and praying,
desperate for the slip
Only then, the feast of human flesh can begin
Try pushing back, the resistance is unmoving, unwavering,
unrelenting, it surrounds us on all sides
Let's pretend we're brave, even though we fear everything; even
what we've earned; even what we truly are
Social chameleons sniping like demons of despair, like monsters
hidden in the closets of unknowing
Wishing we were noticed like the bell of the ball, and hoping
we're invisible all the same

So, they can't see the weakness and cowardice in our eyes or in
our hearts
What is the truth?
Scurry like rats, spreading our virus round another city. If the
atmosphere is the world our streets are the sewer
Crying, loving, fighting, wasting, or rotting
The war is across the seas, the war is in the streets of home, and
mainly, it's inside ourselves
Are we asking the right questions?
Why am I here?
What does it mean?
Or maybe what should I do?
How do we measure success when it means a different thing to
each one of us?
Is it money, is it love, or is it simply the balance between the
laughs and tears?
Is it giving all you are for others, or is it saving some of yourself
for you, is it only you?
Where is the balance?
We're walking razor edges, fearing a terminal slip
We aren't special, we aren't divinity, we aren't gods, we don't
own each other
We don't own the world
We Just get a loan for a lifetime
Do you love?
Civilised humans; maybe we're no more than savages

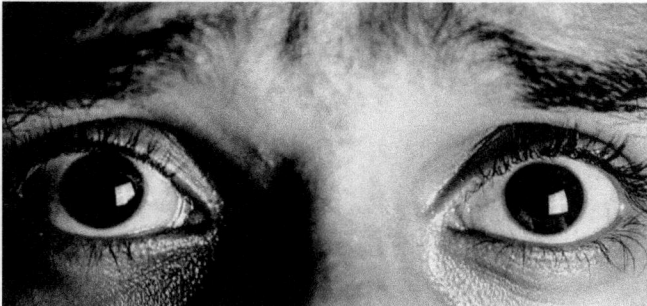

The Land Behind the Eyes   43

Twisted Humans

Time again, just breathing out, the pressure always rising
The blizzard tears up from the south, and you're only just
surviving
Each fallen word, each moments grace, reaching out to touch you
Each stolen smile, in time or space, won't just blindly love you

Each extra weight comes raining down, gravity, endless crushing
With a crooked back, a stricken frown, the soul needs more than
flushing
The mixed-up landscape so far away, confusing and confounding
And now a-drift on the ocean wide, and it feels just like you're
drowning

They take their lump, they cut their slice, the vultures circle
crying
They hope you fall, they want your life, they're hoping that
you're dying
In this body bound, a slave to earth, this crumbled crooked
kingdom
Hard to know just what you're worth, when you're limited by
wisdom

The ghost of grief invades the head, and there forever lingers
The misty haze, the cold regret, reaches out like shadowy fingers
The hope you feel is laced with guilt, the stars mapped up above
you
The folly dreams, the flowers wilt, becomes much harder than it
has to

Silence breaks out once again, with so much still to ponder
A scrambled map that never ends, no matter how you wander

Some ties to cut and some to hold, some ties live inside you
And bridges burn, the fire's cold, and it's setting out to find you

There's no escape, there is no plan, the walls come crashing
round you
False and fake, hard to stand, designed to just confound you
And the howling wind is creeping in, it's voice growls in the
rumble
Wearing thin, unsure, unhinged, a voice that's just a mumble.

Twisted humans, twisted lives, twisted in their meaning
Poisoned darts, twisting knives, to wake you when you're
dreaming
They call their names, and spit the lies, they're weak and those to
pity
Throw their blame, the tensions rise, and it echoes round this
city

They howl and scream and hate you hard, they are in a shell so
empty
They prowl and scheme, wasted hearts, with bitterness and envy
But inside you shine, you light the night, you're tough and fight
for longer
The warmth be thine, it will be fine, when you're only getting
stronger

The flowers bloom, one more time, they'll smile across the
distance
The glowing moon, the sun will shine, on the path of least
resistance
The soul of truth, the enormous heart, know you won't be losing
The hope is here, the day to start, and you'll live it at your
choosing

Love and dance and smile and skip, skip right through tomorrow
Dream and laugh, live a wish, and leave behind the sorrow
Go forward now, glow with pride, always keep believing
You'll spread your joy, where you go, in the dream of which
you're weaving

Peopley

Humans leaving questions, echoes reverberate inside
The shallow swell with ego, the deluded swell with pride
Caution moving onward, out towards the light
Fallen like a snowflake that will break inside a haunted mind

Heart beats rhythm like the thunder, as you wander from your tomb
What the fuck is going on? Are you strong enough for doom?
The shadows spat with fury. They flutter round the room
They linger in the corners, so eager to consume

People so confusing, illusions they like to paint
Acting like a piece of shit, while believing they're a saint
Some take the truth and twist it and throw it in your face
Some hold you in their bloody claws, and won't let you escape

Humans always fucked up, envious and cruel
Emotions send them tumbling, bad reason makes them fall
Fighting for believing, fighting for fuck all
Running hard for freedom, but stuck behind those walls

Anger endless overflowing, through memories that skip
Acting like a monster or acting like a fuckin' prick
Hold onto reason, better hold on to your head
Pat yourself upon the back, for getting out of bed

The cosmos ever drifting, yet keep twisting in their eyes
When you think you've got it figured, you're in for a surprise
Humans always searching, there's no place left to hide
Anyone would think that you can't get out alive

Humans ever probing and prodding at your walls
When you feel like your invincible, they kick you in the balls
When you put your faith in them, just prove that they are fools
Spiteful, growling, spitting, and screaming out their call

People always peopling, and peopley and there
They're swarming all around us. They're fuckin everywhere
There's no way to escape from them. There's hardly anywhere
So chose your people wisely and show them when you care

Losses

Knocking down walls that stand tall and mighty
Taking in souls that are seeking the light
They come, and they stay, and then they move onwards
Some for a week, some for a life

They cry in the night when their heart's cold and lonely
They cry in the night when their strength will run thin
You can give arms to protect them and hold them
And watch one more time as they move on again

Sometimes you lose through anger, through hatred
Sometimes they stay through their greed for your love
Some stay and then hurt you for no fuckin' reason
Sometimes all you got, ain't nearly enough

Some leave your life and move on forever
Some leave your life cos the journey does end
Some were you're family, some of them lovers
Some of them colleagues, some of them friends

We take all the loses whatever their reason
Whether fading away or lost in the night
And for each person that moves on, takes a part of you with
them
The losses will come, but that is this life

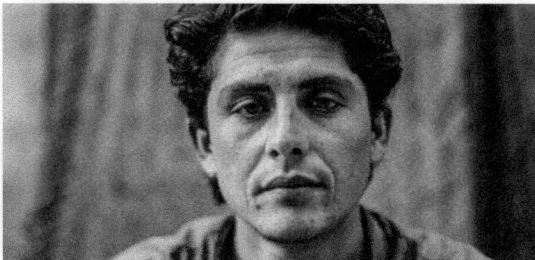

Statuesque

Statuesque
Not quite ready yet to crumble
Frozen solid
Stare into space
Cold as stone
A journey leads to nothing
Cry out the eyes
Or get off the face

Statue boy
The wind does howl around you
You stand in your place
Dumbfounded
Unclear
With your concrete eyes
Focused out to nowhere
With fuzz in your head
And one Stoney tear

Statuesque
Yet no one wants to crumble
Cold wet moss grows
In the cracks on the face
It disappeared
When for a time was hopeful
The ship, smashed on the rocks
It just couldn't steer

Heart of stone
Heavy, and it's bitter
The story short

Connections have flown
Statue boy
Making sense when there's no reason
Statuesque
On this hill alone

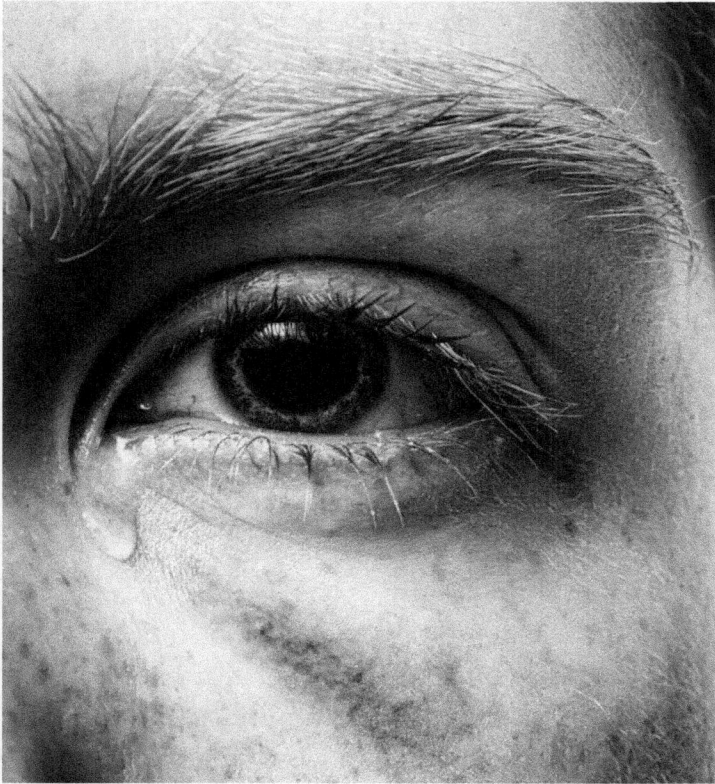

Unashamedly You

The world at times crumbles around you
And everything goes from nothing to cold
The whirlwind is pushing against you
And the fire always sucks out your soul
The breeze shakes the bones, oh so bitter
The trees sway and bow in the wind
The memories flood back one more moment
And you take another punch on the chin
And when everyone around you is fragile
And your strength can't hold out anymore
You'll be twirling and dancing and out of your mind
And you'll roll away like the waves on the shore
And trying and fighting ain't always enough
When the night turns to black from the blue
And you apologise for being so shit and a fool
And being unashamedly you

The flashes right back to the nightmares
That live in your soul not your head
And they fuck you and taunt you, time and again
Until the day that you're happily dead
And the treason on your person so painful
The world so blurry through the tears in your eyes
Get a kick in the head from fuckin' nowhere
And you're not even close to surprised
Just roll with it, keep moving, keep surging
When at times you surge on your knees
You're eating off the scraps off the shit in the bin
And if you ever stop moving you freeze
Keep falling forgotten cold reason
Do you know what is there, what is true?

And you're apologising for being an idiot, a clown
And being unashamedly you

The clouds cross the sky in breeze wild
And they flow as they ride on the wind
The time to forget your cold smile
And wipe off the lost foolish grin
Rain drops like ice fall upon you
Tear drops like floods on your face
The burn in the heart, let's you know you're alive
A walking and talking disgrace
And the voices in your head out to get you
And the echoes that fuck with your mind
And the shadows won't ever forget you
And neither in fact, will the time
The hate in the night may feed us
They just constantly do what they do
And you're sorry for being unstable
And so unashamedly you

But the smiles around you grow brighter
The laughs on the lips of the warm
They will lift you and help you and drive you along
And bring you right in from the storm
The good things you do outnumber
But they are just so hard to see
When darkness surrounds you it's swirling
But one day if you fight you'll be free
Never alone cos you suffer
Suffer from the pain endured
But the pathway has only just started

There's a whole fuckin world to explore
And the walls that surround you will crumble
And you will be like an eagle that flew
Never apologise for being the person you are
Or being unashamedly you

The Revolution

The revolution has begun but you don't need a gun
Grab a hold of your hopes and have a bit of fun
Dancing in the rain or playing in the sun
If this life is just a game, it can honestly be won

Grab yourself a smile and a heart that's full of cheer
If you can do it for a week, you can do it for a year
Knowing that you're beautiful, not running from the fear
Embracing everything you are, through happiness and tears

Spread your love, your wisdom, your warmth and your light
When someone is feeling down, losing their own fight
You can pick them up and help them, watch as they take flight
If you want to, you can do it, it's never may or might

Spreading all the joy til your heart bulges at the seams
You may never know just what it is, but you'll know how much
it means
Let's make smiles from the tears and laughter from the screams
The time has come for you to start, living out those dreams

Be always asking questions and doing all you can
Everyone has got a dream, but they never have a plan
When your eyes and mind are open, there's magic in your hands
You can write your own amazing tune, and also lead the band

Start the morning with a smile and do the things you like
It's called an 'act' of kindness, but it's a way of life
Grab it with all you are, only James Bond's living twice
You want a happy, loving time? It starts by being nice

Wrong

At times you give all, you lose your mind
It hard to just keep breathing
Your energy is wasted now
In a world that is deceiving
You fight for good. You think you should
It's devious and scheming
To rip out that soul, to writhe in a hole
To wake you when you're dreaming

Stand looking out, the empty shout
It's twisting and revolving
And the cracks appear in the atmosphere
And it's time to start evolving
Mistakes were made. The hearts will break
A problem beyond solving
This empty shell, these tears on cheeks
But nowhere near to folding

Look at reflections of the frozen face
The reflections of the story
Sucking strength out of the cosmos now
And thunder to the glory
Take this shot, trembling child
Rage towards your fury
And show your spite, your cowardice
So ugly and so gory

Get it wrong, misreading the signs
Sometimes so misleading
Your shell is hard, but deep inside
The soul is endless bleeding

Give your strength, and words so wise
Keep the vultures feeding
No time to cry, no time to breathe
No moment for your grieving

Hapless hopes, and eyes awoke
Leaves us drowning in our sorrow
The lingering smoke, a heart that's broke
There's no strength left to borrow
The point appears, through hate and fear
Leaves you staring hollow
But you stay on track, do what's right
And keep falling through tomorrow

Get it wrong no matter how right
How beautiful or appalling
The cracks will show, widening more
And towards your fate your falling
Time to start, to carve the path
Be over with your stalling
Head held high, shoulders back
And stumble towards your calling

The Pain

There's so much pain
Everything, it crumbles into piles of dust
Dust that swirls and rolls away in the wind
The cold chill blows across us
The skeletons smash the closet door to pieces
The beautiful, the everything they lose
The ugly is nurtured and stretches endless
Relentless, sucking you in, seducing the souls
The smile is cracked, and false and means fuck all
The creature is real, and true and here to slash us into a million
pieces

There's so much pain
It's ever probing at my frail barriers
It's ever testing the width of these shoulders
If the force of gravity wasn't enough
It wants to crush my fuckin' soul
It tests my defences at every moment from every angle til it's in
The pain is yours, but it is mine
The pain is there again
But the pain will never win

There's so much pain
Let me lift you up, give you hope, give you the words you need
to hear
Let me suck my strength from nothing, let me love you though
you hate yourself
Let me smile at fate inside the mirror
Let me take it on the chin
Let it knock me down, while its friends kick the fuck out of me
on the ground

Cos I'll stand, I'll taste my blood and laugh
You've gotta kill me to fuckin' break me
If this is a fist fight, you better bring a fuckin' tank cos I won't
hide from you

There's so much pain
There's so much shadow in the distance
There's so many raindrops creating floods on the ground
There's so many souls stumbling off the path snarling
Hating through ever-narrowing eyes
Acting like empty fools, while they destroy themselves
Heads spinning, spite-spitting, clowns of shadow sucked inside
the gloom
Crows on the wing, the bird of death, like a shadow circling in
the sky
Wait endless for the victory, for the perceived glory

There's so much pain
But I don't give a fuck about the pain
I'm only bringing light
The pain, a heavy burden, the hope that keeps me strong
There's so much pain
Let it pour all over me, let it reveal itself
It can never slow me down
The pain is out there like an ocean
But so is the joy and so is the love

Uncaged

No welcome for the coward
No respite from the fear
The slipping down the mountainside
And bitter through the tears
The forgotten like a statue
The standing on your own
The cold, the lost, the lonely
The shivers to the bone
The life it zooms by quickly
And it's shouting in your face
Your head is fuckin' spinning round
Your lost, right out of place
You beat yourself so gently
When you cannot find the way
And zip up stay so silent
And don't know what to say
The atmosphere of nothing
The shadow cross the sky
The racing towards a shelter
And sprinting through a life
There's light on the horizon
Are you brave enough to see?
Are you lonesome? are you frightened?
Are you living out your dreams

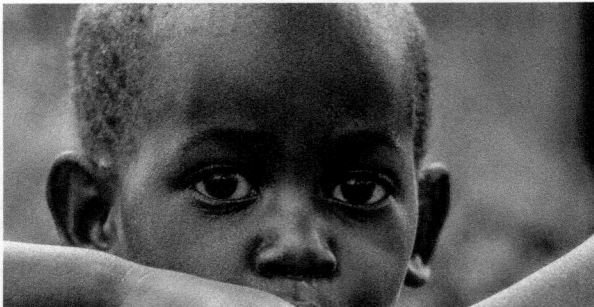

The Forces Within

"Come inside these mists, this shadow
Let me make your blood run cold
Let me consume the joy within you
Then swallow up your soul
Let me invade your mind completely
In the haunted place you know so well
Lurking, ready, hungry
In the darkness where I dwell
Let me break your mind completely
Let me burn down what you made
Let me mock you, taunt you, hurt you
When I sneak up and invade"

"Come to me sweet child
Let me hold you in my arms
You've never been so warm and safe
You won't come to any harm
You are beautiful and smiling
You are waves upon the sea
You will escape the empty prison
You will run and skip so free
Let us dance to life's sweet music
And gaze to the stars above
Let us help a million other souls
And spread around our love"

"Hey fool where you going?
Can't get far from me
I'll hurt you in the waking hours
And haunt you in your dreams
I'm here always inside you

And when you think that I am gone
I'll come back to bite
Just to prove that you are wrong
My duty to your plight is
To always keep a hold
And when you think you are escaping
I will keep control"

"Stay here with me oh sweet one
We can climb the mountains tall
We can jump across the chasm
And scale prison walls
The light flows all around you
And it lives within your blood
It's there to warm your heart
And fill you up with love
You sometimes feel misguided
But you don't get it wrong
The mistakes that never break you
Will only make you strong"

"Here I am, did ya miss me?
I've come to twist the knife
To make you feel so fuckin worthless
That you've had it with this life
I'm gonna scream and hurt you
And tear your soul apart
I'm gonna make you cry
I'll even break your heart
This spirit soon will crumble
And you'll fall down once again
And when you think you've left me
I'm your lifelong friend"

Now I sit in silence
When the hurricane has blown
I stare out upon the ocean
And I know I found my home
I take wonder in the small things
Do all the good I can
Learn what it means to be a human
What it is to be a man
Darkness comes in stages
But I'm drowning it with light
I am a fearsome warrior
And I will win the fight

The End

You shine as brightly as a star in the inky cosmos!

If you enjoyed this book, please leave a review on Amazon or Goodreads today!

Check out: Original and powerful, beautiful and inspiring, take a poetic journey through both outer space and inner, in a thoughtful and uniquely direct way. **Inner Outer: A Poetry Collection.**

For poetry, and wellbeing posts, connect with me on my website **https://bbrunswickpoetry.com**

Other Works

Out Now!

The Land Behind the Eyes: A Poetry Collection

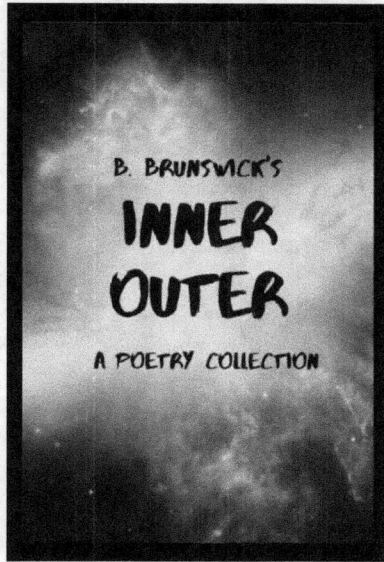

Other Works

Coming Soon!

Here Lies No One: A Poetry Collection

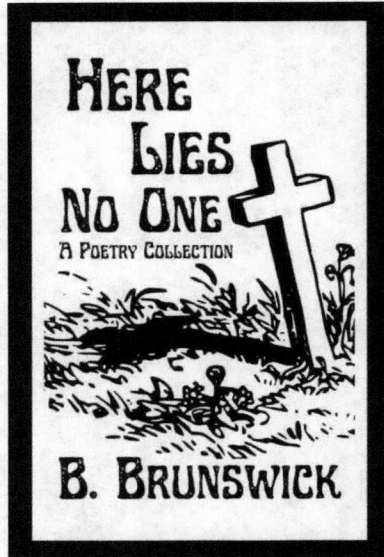

www.ingramcontent.com/pod-product-compliance
Lightning Source LLC
LaVergne TN
LVHW051816080426
835513LV00017B/1976